P9-DMT-333

A Note to Parents

DK READERS is a compelling program for beginning readers, designed in conjunction with leading literacy experts, including Dr. Linda Gambrell, Distinguished Professor of Education at Clemson University. Dr. Gambrell has served as President of the National Reading Conference, the College Reading Association, and the International Reading Association.

Beautiful illustrations and superb full-color photographs combine with engaging, easy-to-read stories to offer a fresh approach to each subject in the series. Each DK READER is guaranteed to capture a child's interest while developing his or her reading skills, general knowledge, and love of reading.

The five levels of DK READERS are aimed at different reading abilities, enabling you to choose the books that are exactly right for your child:

Pre-level 1: Learning to read
Level 1: Beginning to read
Level 2: Beginning to read alone
Level 3: Reading alone
Level 4: Proficient readers

The "normal" age at which a child begins to read can be anywhere from three to eight years old. Adult participation through the lower levels is very helpful for providing encouragement, discussing storylines, and sounding out unfamiliar.words.

No matter which level you select, you can be sure that you are helping your child learn to read, then read to learn!

DK

LONDON, NEW YORK, MUNICH,
MELBOURNE, AND DELHI

Editorial Assistant Ruth Amos
Senior Editor Elizabeth Dowsett
Senior Designer Lynne Moulding
Jacket Designer Lynne Moulding
Pre-production Producer Marc Staples
Producer Charlotte Oliver
Managing Editor Laura Gilbert
Design Manager Maxine Pedliham
Art Director Ron Stobbart
Publishing Director Simon Beecroft

Reading Consultant Dr. Linda Gambrell

Lucasfilm
Executive Editor J. W. Rinzler
Art Director Troy Alders
Keeper of the Holocron Leland Chee
Director of Publishing Carol Roeder

Rovio
Approvals Editor Nita Ukkonen
Senior Graphic Designer Jan Schulte-Tigges
Content Manager Laura Nevanlinna
Vice President of Book Publishing Sanna Lukander

First published in the United States in 2013
by DK Publishing
375 Hudson Street, New York, New York 10014
10 9 8 7 6 5 4 3 2 1

Copyright © 2013 Dorling Kindersley Limited

Angry Birds™ © 2009-2013 Rovio Entertainment Ltd.
All rights reserved.
© 2013 Lucasfilm Ltd. LLC & ® or TM where indicated.
All rights reserved. Used under authorization.

001–193696–June/13

All rights reserved under International and Pan-American
Copyright Conventions. No part of this publication may be
reproduced, stored in a retrieval system, or transmitted in any
form or by any means, electronic, mechanical, photocopying, recording,
or otherwise, without the prior written permission
of the copyright owner.
Published in Great Britain by Dorling Kindersley Limited.

DK books are available at special discounts when purchased in bulk for
sales promotions, premiums, fund-raising, or educational use.
For details, contact:
DK Publishing Special Markets
375 Hudson Street, New York, New York 10014
SpecialSales@dk.com

A catalog record for this book is available
from the Library of Congress.

ISBN: 978-1-4654-0190-8 (Paperback)
ISBN: 978-1-4654-0191-5 (Hardcover)

Color reproduction by Altaimage, UK
Printed and bound in China by L.Rex

Discover more at
www.dk.com
www.starwars.com

Contents

DK READERS

BEGINNING
1
TO READ

ANGRY BIRDS™ STAR WARS™

YODA BIRD'S HEROES

Written by Ruth Amos

The Bird Rebels

The Bird Rebels are
fighting to save the galaxy!

They must defend the galaxy
from the evil pigs.

Chuck
"Ham" Solo

Princess
Stella
Organa

galaxy

Red
Skywalker

Yoda Bird

Yoda Bird is leading his flock
to protect the Bird Republic.

Unlike the pigs, the birds want
to live in peace and harmony.

Terebacca

Obi-Wan Kaboomi

R2-EGG2

C-3PYOLK

The villains

Look out! These are the wicked pigs from the Pig Empire.

The porky pigs want to eat all the candy and junk food in the galaxy.

Pig Pilot

Emperor Piglatine

Pigtrooper

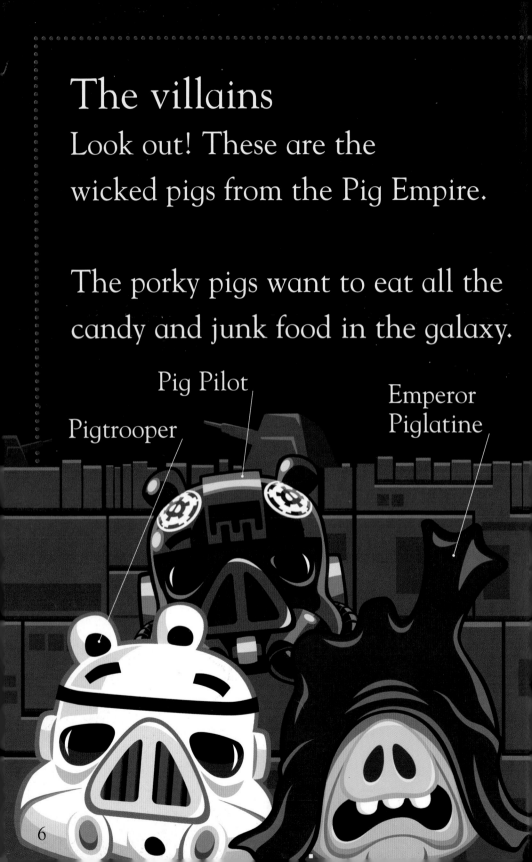

Emperor Piglatine is the evil leader who orders the pigs to attack Yoda Bird and his flock.

Beware this greedy gang!

Lard
Vader

Boba
Fatt

Guard

Snowtrooper

Yoda Bird

This is Yoda Bird, a very wise and old Jedi warrior.

Brave Yoda protects the birds with his lightsaber weapon.

Wrinkly forehead

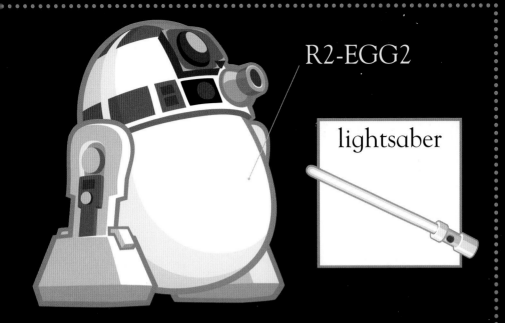

R2-EGG2

lightsaber

Yoda Bird has a secret—
he is the only bird who
knows where The Egg is!

The Egg has the power
to rule the galaxy.

Yoda disguised The Egg as
the robot bird R2-EGG2.

Floppy
hair

Red Skywalker

Red Skywalker is learning
how to be a Jedi warrior,
but he thinks that he knows
everything already!

Red is determined to find
The Egg before the evil pigs
get their hands on it!

It is a pity that Red is so
clumsy—he is always dropping
his lightsaber on the floor and
walking into things!

Jedi
robes

Obi-Wan Kaboomi

Obi-Wan Kaboomi is Red
Skywalker's powerful Jedi Master.

Obi-Wan is very pleased
with his strong Jedi powers.

Brown
cloak

Obi-Wan knows how to do
lots of different tricks with
his blue lightsaber.

Like his leader Yoda, Obi-Wan
uses his lightsaber in battle to
defend the galaxy.

Glowing
lightsaber

Training together

Obi-Wan and Red have lots
of Jedi training classes.

Obi-Wan instructs Red on
proper Jedi behavior.

Obi-Wan talks about his amazing Jedi powers, but sometimes Red does not listen.

Obi-Wan gets annoyed, and Red thinks that his teacher's grumpy face is really funny!

Tuft of feathers

Braided bun

Princess Stella

This is her royal highness,
Princess Stella Organa.

Stella is one of the
most important
Bird Republic leaders
and she works very hard.

squawking

Red and Stella are secretly very jealous of each other's hair.

They have big, squawking arguments over who has the best hairdo.

Stella does not tell Red she wants to swap hair with him!

Chuck "Ham" Solo

This yellow fellow is called Ham and he is a great shot with his blaster.

blaster

He joined the Bird Rebels to help them fight for the Bird Republic.

Ham smuggles junk food around the galaxy in his *Mighty Falcon* starship.

He also uses it to rescue the birds when they are in trouble.

Mighty Falcon

Birds of a feather

Stella and Ham are really good friends.

Sometimes they coo at each other like a pair of lovebirds.

But sometimes Princess Stella gets very angry if Ham disagrees with her!

Watch out, Ham!

Bandolier belt

Terebacca

Terebacca is Ham's biggest, fluffiest friend.

His huge feathers protect him from the cold.

Terebacca grunts and moans instead of talking, but Ham can understand him.

Terebacca and Ham are always laughing and joking about their silly adventures.

Thick feathers

C-3PYOLK

C-3PYOLK is a droid bird,
with a shiny golden body.

C-3PYOLK is a robot of peace,
who squawks all day long
about staying out of trouble.

C-3PYOLK wants
to stop the battles
between the birds
and the pigs.

droid

This is because fighting
makes C-3PYOLK nervous!

Big, wise
eyes

R2-EGG2

R2-EGG2 does not know he is the disguise for The Egg!

The Egg is very powerful because it contains the Force.

Camera eye

The Force is a power
that can rule the galaxy.

R2-EGG2 is a droid bird,
like his friend, C-3PYOLK.

R2-EGG2 always tries to look
after C-3PYOLK.

Red
Skywalker
pilot

Flyboys

Red Skywalker and the
rest of his squadron
are amazing pilots!

They zoom along
at top speed in their
X-wing Birdfighters.

Sometimes they fly so fast
that it makes them dizzy.

R2-EGG2 sits in the back of
Red's Birdfighter to help him fly
and save the galaxy.

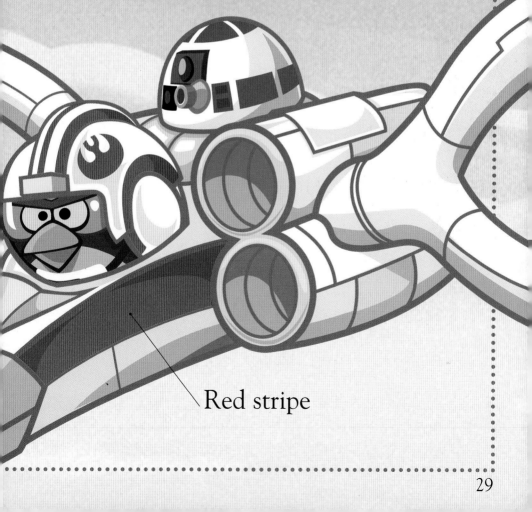

Red stripe

TIE fighter

Space battle

These sinister swine are attacking the Bird Rebels.

The pigs launch their TIE fighter aircraft through the air.

Yoda leads
his flock into
battle, and the
birds fight back bravely.

The Bird Rebel heroes have
saved the galaxy—this time!

Glossary

Blaster
A weapon that shoots out laser blasts.

Droid
A robot.

Galaxy
A group of stars and planets.

Lightsaber
A sword-like weapon that has a beam made of pure energy.

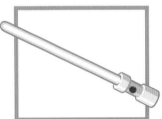

Squawking
A harsh, shrieking noise that birds make.